A Life
We Never Dared
Hope For

A Life
We Never Dared
Hope For

(Vivre l'inespéré)

Journal 1972–1974

by

BROTHER ROGER OF TAIZÉ

MOWBRAY
LONDON & OXFORD

Copyright © Presses de Taizé 1980

ISBN 0 264 66718 2

First published in English 1980
by A. R. Mowbray & Co Ltd,
Saint Thomas House,
Becket Street,
Oxford, OX1 1SJ

Originally published in France under the title
Vivre l'inespéré 1976, 1978
Translated by Emily Chisholm
and the Taizé Community

Printed in Great Britain by
Fletcher & Son Ltd, Norwich

Contents

There is a Life . . .   *page* 7
Journal: 5 April–15 July 1972   10

The essential hidden from our eyes   21
Journal: 19 July 1972–4 March 1973   26

Who can condemn us?   35
Journal: 7 March–24 October 1973   38

From doubt towards believing   47
Journal: 26 October 1973–6 April 1974   51

Loved with Eternity's love   61
Journal: 8 April–30 August 1974   64

A life we never dared hope for   73

DEDICATED TO
KONGCHEE SAE-UNG
AND
MENGHOH SAE-URE

THERE IS A LIFE . . .

There is a Life . . .

There is a Life hidden in man, a Life which rouses his hope. It opens a way forward, the way of a becoming, for each person and for all humanity.

Will you focus your attention on it?

Without this hope, anchored at the very heart of your heart, without this becoming stretched out beyond yourself, you lose any desire to forge ahead.

No sheer projection of your own wishes, but a hope which leads you to live in ways which seemed to lie beyond all hope, even in situations with no issue.

Alone before Christ you will have the courage to wait for the course of history, even at its most ineluctable, to burst wide open.

This hope produces surging creativity, which overturns all the determinisms of injustice, hatred, and oppression.

Alone before Another, hope given by him. Hope that invents the world anew.

When you let your world revolve around yourself, you are plunged into self-centredness, all your powers of creation and love dislocated.

To displace this centre, and for love to be kindled there, you are offered the same fire offered to every person in the world – his Spirit in you.

His impetus, his spontaneity, his inspiration have only to waken, for life to become intense and real.

8

In the vanguard of the Church, will you be a carrier of living waters? Will you quench the thirst of all who are searching for the source?

Peace and justice are not served merely by the desire for them. It is still essential to go to the source and reconcile in oneself struggle and contemplation.

Could anyone willingly consent to be a mere conformist in prayer, justice or peace? Could anyone freely let it be said of him: He talks but he does not act, says 'Lord, Lord', but does not do his will; he says 'Justice, justice', but does not practise it; he says 'Peace, peace', but within there is war?

Many others as well as yourself are haunted by this question. Fervent seekers after Christ in contemplation, they pay the price of justice and of peace with their own lives.

These words, spoken by young Asians, ring in my ears, 'In the past, forms of prayer imported from abroad shaped us in ways that took no account of our own native genius; now it is programmes of justice worked out elsewhere which are being imported, sometimes several rival ones – from conformist models of prayer to conformist models of justice!'

In prayer and in the search for justice, saying without doing would make you one of the oppressors.

Never let yourself be trapped in the alternative, either commitment to the oppressed or the quest for sources.

Not struggle or contemplation, but both together, one springing from the other.

This radicalism of the Gospel demands too much for you to pass judgement on those who do not understand.

Even if you are not understood, do not stand still. You are the one to take this risk.

A hand to grasp your own, to lead you out along the way? No one can do that for another . . .

Only he who has recognised you already . . .

JOURNAL: 5 APRIL–15 JULY 1972

5 April 1972

I would go to the ends of the earth if necessary, to the
farthest reaches of the globe, to speak over and over
again of my confidence in the new generations, my confidence in the young.

We who are older have to listen, and not condemn.
Listen, to grasp the creative intuitions alive within them.

They are blazing trails, they are overturning barriers,
they will take the whole People of God along with them.
The young will find a way beyond the demarcation-lines
which now divide believers from believers, they will
invent means of communion uniting believers with non-
believers.

As for the old, I am convinced that without them, the
world would not be worth living in. Those societies,
families or churches which exclude them do not know
what they are doing.

Old people who accept their approaching death acquire
irreplaceable powers of intuition. They understand with
the understanding of the heart. By their loving trust they
make it possible for the young, and the not-so-young, to
become truly themselves; with their ability to discern the
best in others, they release unsuspected sources of life in
them.

Every rift between generations works against the sense of the universal.

6 *April*
God is so bound up with mankind that wherever there is a human being, God is present, whether we want him or not.

7 *April*
Two years ago, we chose to begin the preparation of the Council of Youth with an 'inner adventure'. That meant going against the stream: nowadays people are only too ready to make do with short-term commitments, with resolves that scarcely last out the week.

Let the living water of Christ's presence come surging up within us, and a whole inner world comes into being, filling the voids. We are borne far beyond all the oppressive ways of life that characterise our civilised societies.

Refuse the freshness offered by the Gospel? Never! However fleeting, it is the happiness of the Beatitudes, the wellspring of poetry, of imagination, and of the ability to kindle flame with the hardest of wood: even broken relationships, or the death of someone we love, can be used to light glowing fires.

Once launched on this adventure, we realise that it does not stop at ourselves; if it were kept private, it would turn against us. Even at the very beginning, it opens the way irresistibly to encounter with others; it drives us on to a high hill crowned by a 'city with her lights shining for all to see'.

For the past two years, we have been embarking on an inner adventure, which sustains our vocation to be universal – to be present for everybody.

But who does not dread this inner adventure? It is unsettling; it has the savour of wild fruit, those unexpected finds round a bend in the road. It opens up ways we never dreamed of, paths we had never hoped to find.

8 April

With one of my brothers, called on Father Buisson. His face shines with peace and mercy; he is gazing at the invisible already. Whoever would have thought it? He is eighty-six, and in a way he has replaced John XXIII in my life.

At the age of forty, he still could not make up his mind to be ordained, so strong were his scruples, his feelings of guilt and inferiority. 'That taught me to understand the people who come to unburden their souls to me.'

Still listening, I rise to do what he can no longer do himself: taking three glasses from the cupboard, I pour out the sweet wine and pass round the few biscuits he buys for us when we come.

He asserts that, as far as he can see, his ministry has borne no fruit. When God takes him back to himself, he will know all that his priesthood has achieved.

3 May

These last three days, the heat has penetrated the farthest corners. Leaning against the edge of the open window, I listen to all the little noises rising from the wood below.

The pansies have faded already, earlier than usual. By the trough, one or two yellow tulips are still in flower. On both sides of them, cascading down the wall a few yards from my window, are trails of tiny wild flowers, splashes of white and-mauve on the other side of the gap which separates us.

5 May

G. has just arrived from Brazil. He is the only priest for a parish of twenty-eight thousand people near Recife. Infantile mortality is high; children sometimes hold the funeral services for other children, among themselves, with no adults present. Sometimes a husband has to bury his wife himself.

10 May

A South American Indian leader, visiting us, tells how his brother was killed defending other workers. His attackers clubbed him down viciously, then ran over his body with a truck. His ability to bear his own brother's death and still be eager to help the downtrodden, he attributes to his parents' faith. He asks: How could I truly say I love God, if I do not actively love my brothers? How can I reconcile violent struggle against those who are oppressing my Indian brothers and sisters with the call of the Gospel?

20 May

Why not receive communion at the Catholic Eucharist? It seems everything is ready for it.

21 May

Pentecost. Two brothers return from a month spent in Spain. In Galicia and the Asturias they found young people isolated to the point of abandonment – fear strangling their lives. Weep, beloved of God.

Father Arrupe visits us. Not so very long ago, the mere mention of the General of the Jesuits was enough to strike terror into certain hearts. Today, this man is the John XXIII of his order; he is one of the signs of springtime in the Church.

23 May

Tuesday after Pentecost. A road accident a few kilometres away has cost a boy his life.

After the midday prayer, I went to see the driver of the minibus; he was sitting in a corner of the church on a low stool. His eyes were bright, clear as deep waters before a storm. Neither of us spoke. I stood there with one hand resting on his bowed head. The other people who had been in the bus when the accident happened gradually gathered round; they had not been told that Hans-Peter had died on the way to the hospital. But as they came up, our silence made them realise. I began to pray, with others following in a long, restrained litany.

Later they explained that Hans-Peter, a seventeen-year-old electrical engineer, had only very recently found his way to the faith. The boy who had been driving the bus was the one who had been closest to him during that time.

3 June

Anniversary of the death of Pope John XXIII. A man capable of looking beyond the immediate situation, he never let himself be upset by warnings that the worst was bound to happen. Three months before he died, two of my brothers and I saw him in tears because his real intentions were being misrepresented. It was the hardest trial of all for him, but he never let himself be caught in that kind of snare. At eighty-two, he surmounted all the obstacles set in his way and succeeded in issuing his last encyclical, *Pacem in terris*. There were any number of attempts to prevent its publication, shortly before his death; but he managed to see it through. In that too he was the universal pastor: taking risks with and ahead of the flock, making no reply to his detractors.

In old age, John XXIII showed the qualities of a true leader. Others might distort his most disinterested intentions, but he never fell into the trap set for him. He looked beyond the numerous pressures being brought to bear. If he had based his decisions on reaction to them, he would have been unable to fulfil his charge. If he had begun to justify himself, he would have been bound hand and foot. The best way to make the sense of his actions clear was to go still further in the same direction.

4 June

After today's showers the air is cool, refreshing the very soul. Over on the hills towards Tournus, the gentle evening light changes from moment to moment. Down in the valley, cars speeding along: all homeward bound.

14

5 June

Evening spent with a young couple, active in a trade union. Their struggle is at a low ebb and they feel lost. They find themselves ignored by so many of the younger workers, whose main concern seems to be to improve their financial situation. So we search: what ways are there of overcoming the obstacles? In any passionate search there come times of despondency. There is a future beyond their present situation. And it is clear to them where new birth lies.

7 June

This Saturday, H. and J.B., a couple living in the village, are celebrating their fiftieth wedding anniversary. So we gathered around them today in the little church. They were with us when we first began, and they shared in our adventure. For years, it was in their kitchen and downstairs room that our guests had their meals. We have gone through so much together.

11 June

Just before leaving on a journey, I spend a few minutes with Edith and her husband. It is almost forty years since we last saw one another. She was already engaged when my parents sent me to board at her mother's. She reminds me how, in those months, I spent most of the time talking to her mother, so that she felt rather inferior. Actually I felt intimidated by her seriousness, mistaking it for arrogance!

It was her family, I remind her, that gave me the opportunity of absorbing the Catholic faith. Do you remember, Edith, your mother's devotion to the Eucharist? When she was overwhelmed with difficulties, there she found light.

At the close of our conversation, I left to catch the train, and in my heart we went on talking. Do you remember, Edith, the Epiphany celebrations on 6 January in 1929 or 1930? Those festive hours challenged and stirred me. Now Epiphany has become one of the chief festivals at Taizé.

21 June

This evening there was a television programme when young people were given the chance to express themselves freely. That in itself is a breath of fresh air, even though what they have to say is not all of equal value. Why am I so grateful? Because when I was young, I too met with indifference when I tried to raise objections to things which were generally accepted – to the conformist attitude of Christians divided into various denominations, for example. The inertia seemed so great that I sometimes used to tell myself: accept that in your own lifetime you will not see any results from your life's commitment. That may be why today I am so sympathetic towards those who are young. How many of them will succeed in sharing with others the purity of their intentions?

29 June

Fatima is here, come to see me with other children. For the last few weeks, the face of this little Portuguese girl has worn an expression known only to angels. I begin to tell her a story, making it up as I go along. Her eyes, like two great motionless pearls, listen more than her ears do. She sits bolt upright, quite still. Calm sometimes precedes a storm; before violent hurricanes nature halts, and there is not the slightest breath stirring.

3 July

In my room, a group from Finland. All Protestants, they have travelled the length and breadth of their country to link up all those preparing the Council of Youth there. The group is led by a married couple. Taisto, the husband, is silent, blond and energetic, a man of the Far North; he lets Anna-Maija, his wife, do the talking. She is a poet and a writer, brimming over with energy. From time to time he adds something to what she is saying. They point out in an atlas the places where young people meet. There is one on the shores of Lake Inari, north of the Arctic Circle. As the words flow, a tinge of the midnight sun creeps into our eyes; wild scents, stunted lichens surround us for a fleeting moment.

4 July

Evening spent with members of my family. After a period of weakness, my mother is livelier than ever. Paul, her grandson, had brought some flowers he picked this morning two hundred kilometres from here, near the house where she was born. She begins to recall childhood memories she has never told before, and a song she has not sung since her youth. Her face shines with the infinite dignity of long life and poetic joy.

5 July

All morning long, pouring rain. The waterlogged garden breaks into a symphony of colours. It was not enough for me to see the rain through glass. As soon as I could spare a moment from work, I ran out to the porch to listen to the drops steadily drumming on the roof. Close by, an umbrella opened and a voice grumbled, 'What miserable weather!' Can people be so blind to beauty?

At every stage of life we are granted new harmony. Why dread our failing powers when the years bring inner vision and life gentle as breath? The breath of the Holy Spirit? Is that the soul – the secret heartbeat of a bliss beyond words?

A day is rounded when it is like a whole lifetime in miniature. Every moment has its own intensity. Recover the astonishment of each of the fourteen hundred and forty minutes that every day contains. Recover the wonder of these two little pebbles Marc gave me years ago. The smaller is quite flat and dark, with pale streaks. There is a circle at its centre.

Every day can bring disappointments, attacks, bitter cups to drink: they are all pitfalls ready to stifle our sense of wonder. Above all, every day offers the expectation of His coming.

A day is round and vast when the worst does not succeed in smothering that Breath of fullness.

6 July

A girl writes, telling me her distress after the break-up of her relationship with a boy: 'The break is heart-rending for me, but I cannot hold it against him. All the other relationships I have, and there are many, are not able to keep me from tasting the full tragedy of human isolation. I have not often felt it so strongly. Only Another can give peace.'

Her distress has deep roots. It began in the brutality of a father who perhaps never loved her – at least that is what she feels.

7 July

This day, Patriarch Athenagoras enters the life of eternity. With him we lose a man of the same prophetic vein as John XXIII.

He had no lack of trials in his last years. He had realised what changes were necessary in the People of God, but with the situation as it was, he was obliged to suppress the best of his intuitions. Notwithstanding, he was always optimistic. 'In the evening, when I retire to my room,' he told me once, 'I close the door on all my cares, and I say: Tomorrow!'

I cannot forget the words he spoke twice when I last visited him in Constantinople, two years ago: 'I am going to make my confession to you; you are a priest. I could receive the Body and Blood of Christ from your hands.' Then the next day: 'I could confess to you.' As we took our leave, he added these other words, standing in the doorway and making with his hands the gesture of raising the chalice: 'The cup and the breaking of bread. There is no other solution; remember.'

Engraved on my memory, too, is a pilgrimage Max and I made with him around Constantinople during an earlier visit. Every time our car passed a spot where a Christian had died for Christ, he asked the driver to slow down or stop. We made the sign of the cross, then drove on.

11 July
The newspapers are hopeful that in three weeks' time there will be a peace settlement in Vietnam. The fiery nightmare will be over. If I were ever tempted to forget the drama of Vietnam, the eyes of the young Vietnamese now at Taizé would be enough to remind me: day after day those eyes reflect all too well what their people are going through.

15 July
The essential is always hidden from our eyes . . . and that lends still more ardour to the quest, and sustains our advance towards the only reality.

This thought, much in my mind these past few days, might make a good heading for my next book . . .

THE ESSENTIAL HIDDEN
FROM OUR EYES

The essential hidden from our eyes

The person who prays has a guiding star. Like a hidden, invisible pole, it draws him on. Frequently he is obliged to feel his way, but the goal he has in view fills his whole being, leading him along.

Step by step he discovers that he has been created to be the dwelling-place of Another than himself. As he begins to listen to what is happening in his heart of hearts, he understands that he is unique. Through his poor praying, he is touched to the very roots; he becomes another person for other people.

A life from elsewhere
Prayer is both struggle and surrender. Prayer is also waiting, waiting for a way through, waiting for the walls of our inner resistance to break down. In the same way, Christ in his earthly life knew times of intense patience.

Prayer is an astonishing thing. It propels us elsewhere, out of ourselves. Christ is recognised in our neighbour, to be sure, and he is always alive within us; but he is elsewhere too, present in his own right.

Prayer is always poor, we who live it are poor servants to the very end. Prayer will always exceed our powers. Words are unfit to describe it. In prayer there lies something beyond what we are, beyond our own words.

For all of us, meaning in language is so important. It is easy to understand that, on approaching this fluid realm where everything seems to happen in the incommunicable, the first reaction of many is repulsion or fear.

It was so from the very beginnings of Christian history: 'We do not know how to pray, but the Holy Spirit comes to the help of our inadequacy, he prays in us.'

Prayer never changes in its essence through the centuries, but it adopts different forms as history unfolds, or at different periods of our lives.

Some pray with no words. All is wrapped in a great silence.

Others use very many words to express themselves. In the sixteenth century Teresa of Avila, a woman of great courage and realism, wrote of prayer, 'When I speak to the Lord, I often do not know what I am saying. It is love that speaks. And the soul is so beside itself that I can see no difference between it and God. Love forgets itself and says foolish things.'

Others find in the liturgy, or in common prayer, the joy of heaven on earth, a fulfilment . . .

There are some who repeat over and over again a few words they have learned to stammer. Through this prayer of repetition, a prayer suitable for the poor – and we are all of us poor – the whole being is brought into unity. Some repeat the humble greeting of Elizabeth to Mary, 'Hail Mary . . .' Those may be the only words they have left when they are caught off their guard by human distress. Or else they murmur, audibly or not, to the rhythm of their breathing, the prayer of the Name of Jesus. To all appearances, the endless repetition of the same words lacks spontaneity. Yet, after long waiting, life comes surging up within, a fullness, the Holy Spirit's unsettling presence.

What of those others who practically never experience any detectable resonance of a presence in them? Their whole life long, they are in waiting and that is the fire behind their seeking. Contemplation is a struggle, it does not bring immediate fullness flooding over them, it does not arouse any spontaneous outburst of feeling for Christ.

Many are the ways of prayer. Some follow one, others pursue them all. There are moments of bright certainty – Christ is there, speaking within us. But there are other moments when he is Silence, a distant Stranger . . . No one is privileged in prayer.

In all its infinite variety, prayer brings us across to a life not our own, a life from elsewhere.

Another's looking

What distinguishes a person who builds his entire life on the challenge of prayer from somebody who is indifferent to it? To the outward eye, nothing. The person who prays is the same as everyone else, getting up each morning, walking around, eating ... But within, there is all the difference in the world. For that person, the challenge of prayer is a creation more essential than the events of his own history.

If prayer were aimed at some practical goal, what a mockery it would be! Nothing but a projection of self, even a bargaining-match with God!

Whether serene contemplation or inner struggle, prayer is just learning to place everything in other hands, with the simplicity of a child.

Through the steadfastness of prayer, each one finds energy for other struggles – for maintaining his family or for transforming social conditions ... Far from withdrawing or escaping from events and from people, he now considers them with eyes informed by Another's looking.

When someone is desperately self-seeking, when he cannot tear his eyes away from himself, the pride of life sweeps him along with its inevitable accompaniment of ambition, careerism and the longing to be a success. But if, on the contrary, he lets Another use his eyes, then nothing but the unique reality will count.

Everything depends on how we look at ourselves, other people and events. So much so, that almost everything that happens to us arises out of ourselves. Either the pride of life is the driving-force of our existence, and all that counts is domination of people and things, by money but also without money. Or Christ's looking takes the place of our own. Then the way lies open for the gift of our lives.

The gateways of praise

Someone dear to me gave me an account one day of a whole inner battle:

'I have known what it is to be tempted by self-analysis – all its question-marks, its incessant who-are-you's and its endless whys. This sort of questioning can sometimes lead to vanity, but more often than not the result is sadness, shame and self-contempt. So I kept turning over the earth of my being, working at it in an attempt to make it more and more beautiful, until in the end I had made the beauty of my earth a goal in itself, forgetting that the aim is to sow a seed of Gospel in it.

'I knew the words in Isaiah, "You shall call your gateways praise". But I called mine introspection, anguish and scruple. On my gateways was written, "I am no more worthy to be called your son". Those are narrow gates, not opening outwards at all, but inwards to the lowest levels of the self.

'From now on I shall call my gateways praise. Those gates open wide towards the outside world, towards him who is beyond all things and beyond myself.'

When introspection and analysis turn a man in on himself, what destruction that brings! Who then will open for him the gateways of praise?

Shortly before he died in 1943, a political prisoner in southern Spain, Miguel Hernandez, unveiled a certain secret:

> Open, Love, in me the gates
> of the perfect wound;
> Open, to release
> the useless anguish;
> Open, see, coming,
> the breath of your word.

The gateways of praise give passage to deathly anguish and to songs unending. God will set his mark on the very wounds themselves, making them no longer torment, but energy for communion.

To want a life with no contradictions, shocks, opposition, with no criticism, is to fall into disincarnate dreaming. Confronted by the shaking of foundations, in ourselves, in the Church or in human society, we are offered two ways.

Either hurt and anguish pass into bitterness, when, groaning under the crushing load, we become rooted to the spot and all is lost.

Or else pain and sadness find an outlet in the praise of His love, lifting us out of passivity and enabling us to deal with anything that comes our way.

JOURNAL: 19 JULY 1972–4 MARCH 1973

19 July

The last remnants of harvest languish under the burning rays of the midday sun. All is ready for the festival of the summer nights. The long, phosphorescent dragonflies still hide under the sycamore leaves; soon they will be soaring into their frantic dance.

Now the birds have fallen silent. The only perceptible noise comes from the engines of the mill down by the Grosne, working continuously. The headlights of its lorry stab through the darkness.

21 July

Visit of Dom Fragoso. Small, like the peasants of his region of Brazil, this bishop has the strength of conviction common to all who live in the North-East.

He speaks strong language; he has radical things to say about European aid to Latin America. No matter how generously meant, it is for him the sign of how dependent the countries of the Southern world still are. It is too easy for Latin America to go on accepting European experts; it would be better to train more of their own people. He sees the same pattern in the Church: it is easier for a bishop to call on foreign priests than to train men on the spot. He agrees that certain people, well suited to Latin America, can act as forerunners. But they will have to be ready, like John the Baptist, to step down so that those born locally can grow up.

22 July
X. has been obliged to leave the country he lived in. He bears the marks of his forced departure; his eyes are still full of the horror of the events he witnessed.

'I saw two of my friends,' he says, 'African priests, led away in handcuffs. When they were about to be shot, they asked for the handcuffs to be taken off so that they could announce the liberation of forgiveness and give absolution to all those condemned with them. Then they began to sing, and fell under bullets fired by their own countrymen.'

Leaving me, he concludes, 'Pray, and do something. They are on their own. World opinion knows nothing.'

23 July
This morning, one of the people waiting to see me is a young mother. With a great deal of difficulty, she tells me about the death of her only son, Pierre; he was ten. My breath fails as I try to say, 'You are still young. I shall go ahead of you into God's eternity. There I will speak to Pierre, I promise. Why, even now, Pierre knows that we are here together.'

O heart of my soul, weep for the sorrows of all those people I met today! It is He who has to open the way. On the rocky path my step stumbles . . . Dare to go on, never looking backwards, on towards wonder, on past hoping.

Suppose that the ultimate meaning of life were the joy of God in us all?

24 July
Above my mantelpiece, the icon of the Virgin in the evening shadows. The lamp before it reveals the outlines of Virgin and Child.

Since the death of Athenagoras, this icon has gained in importance. I remember how the Patriarch of Constantinople insisted that Max and I choose an icon for Taizé from his cathedral. Embarrassed by the gesture, we accepted the most dilapidated icon we could find, even if it had to be restored later.

An icon dimly lit! In the darkness of every Christian's life, a light reveals the outlines of beings and things, and the night glows with a flame that never goes out.

31 July

Midday meal with young Africans. Improvisation certainly did play a trick on us today! Life is made simpler if things are not over-organised, but we must accept the consequences. Certainly the table had been pulled out to its full length, but the sheet used as a tablecloth had not been ironed, and the meal was a frugal one. Paper-thin slices of ham! And all that was left in the kitchen was bread to fill the baskets!

2 August

Events in China . . . So many books and articles about that country read enthusiastically over the past twenty years. The brutality of the political upheavals which China has undergone throughout the centuries makes its people all the more attractive. I wonder if the new possibilities of exchange and communication will at last lift the veil which time after time seems doomed to drop?

23 August

Laid down my pen to greet a young trade unionist from the steel industry. Two words in our conversation stand out: struggle and contemplation. All Christian political involvement is set between those two poles. He speaks with consuming passion of his struggle to free others from every form of oppressive power – not only the power of economic forces, but also at times the power wielded by hidebound trade-unions. He is convinced that situations where human beings are most oppressed produce contemplatives – people capable of living, above all else, the love of Christ.

2 September
The rays of the setting sun shine golden in one corner of the room, where a vase of autumn flowers has stood since yesterday. Constantly, as I work, my eyes stray over it.

5 September
Massacre at Munich. A young novice on his way through here remarks: The Palestinians have really played it well at Munich! One of my brothers, also young, asks him: Can murder, wherever it comes from, ever really win our support? That young novice had given his without hesitating.

28 September
Visit from Pablo Cano and his wife. Their faces, Andalusia itself! Such eloquent eyes! They have come to ask me if I will say a few words to the family and give my blessing at the wedding of their daughter Adelaida. At home, they say, it is always the head of the family who gives his blessing. Here, you are our family.

29 September
Went for an hour's outing with a young man from Togo. On the way back, we stop for a moment in the tiny oratory belonging to the sisters in Ameugny. We had only meant to spend a couple of minutes there, but the sisters insist that we come in, and we find ourselves in their living room. The two windows look westward, towards the setting sun, a glowing ball lighting up ashen clouds. A large Bible is open on the floor.

I suggest that our African guest read aloud a prayer, written by a believer long ago, in the Old Testament:

'Two things I ask, do not refuse them before I die. Take from me falsehood and lying. Give me neither poverty nor wealth. Let me enjoy my share of bread. In abundance, I might betray you and say, there is no God. In deprivation I might steal, and so profane the name of the Lord.'

7 October

Marseilles. Went to pray down in the crypt of St Victor's church, where Christians have been gathering ever since the third century. Emerging from the crypt, we find a wedding in progress, a young African couple. The bride is covered in veils and lace. The priest invites the sparse congregation to come and greet the newlyweds. I come forward and say that I will greet them in place of their mothers and fathers. They tell me their names: Marie-Claude and Alex.

9 October

As the years go by, my brothers' parents become increasingly close and dear to me. Anthony's mother and father are here. I see them walking beneath the trees. At once I leave the young couple I was talking to, and run out to them. Spontaneously I embrace them, forgetting that this is an unusual gesture for English people. We make for my room. The conversation is more than I had imagined. Anthony is their only son, so I would have liked to end by telling them that, whatever life may bring, we will always support them in every way. But I could not pronounce the words.

25 October

Father Buisson has come to us. He is eighty-six and it had been agreed that when he was no longer able to live alone, he would come and live in our house. He is very weak, and spends the day sitting by the fire in our common room. His life has known much inner struggle;

it is easy to see what makes people of his calibre irreplaceable.

This priest, with all his experience, makes me think of
the message Daniel's aged mother wrote for her children
before she died: 'Do not be sad to see me go, but steep
yourselves in thankfulness for all that God gives you day
after day. Concentrate on what is going well.'

5 November

In Florence, with Dom Helder Camara. We have to
speak twice, first in a square and then in a stadium
during a Mass. I have spent long hours working to be
able to say in Italian all that I had prepared.

Any event of this kind is a trial, and first I had said no.
But a chance to say what I think about the way money is
used in the Church is worth seizing. It is not the speaking which is a trial, but the mass gathering, all the noise
associated with a great crowd.

Eleven years of friendship with Dom Helder! The
better we know each other, the more our meetings are
like those of two little children.

My room has a view of the Duomo. I had never seen it
by night before, subtly illuminated. The floodlights
caressing its sumptuous architecture surround it with a
vast grey, hazy cloud, the billowing incense of the three
Wise Men.

7 November

On the way back from Florence, stopped in Romain-
motier to listen to the new organ in the church. Warm,
fraternal welcome from the pastor, an old friend. A festive meal at his table. He and his wife are attentive to
every detail, and this expression of a united couple says
more than all their words. The church's stonework
shimmers in hazy sunlight. Music makes the fullness
which is in God more accessible – as though the heavens
were rent and a few notes from the invisible slipped
through.

11 November

Dancing light sparkles on the nasturtiums hanging down over the trough. Warmth in the mid-November air. People say, 'The seasons are not what they used to be.' Certainly, with the roses still blooming, you begin to wonder.

20 November

Return after two days in London. A meeting in a poor part of town with young people from every region of England, with a few of their pastors. The meeting ended with a public service in St Paul's Cathedral. It was quite something, in that venerable church, to see the young people sitting on the floor on their coats and blankets, celebrating the Resurrection with a little candle in their hands!

Afterwards, I have a conversation with the Archbishop of Canterbury. He is a man close to the sources. Many young people are looking forward to his visit to Taizé next year. We expect prophetic words from him.

1 December

Departure for Rome. December is already here, but the morning sunlight is so strong that the lime trees cast deep shadows across the green grass. The last roses are gleaming. To be forced to leave these skies . . .

2 December

First evening in Rome. Go for a walk as far as the Piazza Navona, lined with stalls. One has rag dolls for sale; I choose one with a red blouse, a flat, laughing face and long, dangling legs, to take home as a present for one of the children. The young stall-keeper is surprised: we met at Taizé last summer.

9 December

Last night at eight, conversation with the Pope. Paul VI had carefully read the report in which I had tried to

analyse certain characteristic trends of present-day consciousness. My question was: how to face up to these
trends and not reject them? Or, in the Gospel's language,
how not to abolish but to fulfil?

After our conversation, we went to the chapel for a
simple prayer and a moment of silence. 'I know how fond
of silence you are at Taizé,' the Pope says.

Our conversation continues over the meal. My heart is
full on finding the Pope so able to understand the way
young people think. As we part, he insists, 'If you have
the key for understanding the young, tell me what it is.'

I would like to have that key, but I know that I do not
have it, and never shall.

24 January 1973

The day is dying on the bare earth in the garden below. Six
in the evening. Another few minutes, and the owl will begin
to call its fellows with long, repeated cries. Grégoire drops
in for a moment, we speak a few words, and night has
fallen. Yan's two windows shine like two pale eyes.

28 January

Paris. Night of prayer in St Ignace. Those who like improvisation must have been satisfied. At the start, the
church was so packed that the young people still in the
street outside had to be invited to come back later, when
others had left.

This morning, the skies of Paris reflected our joy at
being alive. Four of us crossed the Seine by the Pont des
Arts, then went into the Tuileries Gardens. Distant per-
spectives opened around the Arc de Triomphe and the
high-rise blocks beyond. That was our morning's goal:
foreground blending into background, harmonious pro-
gressions added century after century by human hands.

21 February

A brother receives a phone-call from the mayor of a
nearby village. Recently a childless widow died there,

and on opening her will the lawyer discovered that she had left her house and estate to our community. We wrote quickly to say that we refused this bequest, in the same way as the community has always refused to accept gifts.

27 February

At his weekly audience last Wednesday, Pope Paul referred to our life here. Talking about the young, he stressed how many of the young people at Taizé seek silence.

2 March

On the post, a letter from a woman who writes to thank me for *Festival*. The mother of three young children, she is seriously ill. She reads to calm the anguish when her family leaves her at the end of visiting time. She concludes:

'Today my children arrived and said: here is a bit of spring for you. The smallest of the girls was hidden behind a whole branch of forsythia. So I am sending you a twig of it in advance for your birthday, because by that time I shall no doubt be myself in the festival that has no end.'

4 March

In church this morning, after I had talked with a number of people, a little girl came up and asked, 'Could you teach me how to confess?' There was a burden weighing on her frail shoulders. How can an eight-year-old child be so imprisoned in guilt? 'Who can condemn us, since Jesus is praying for us?' I intend to make my Easter morning sermon a meditation on those words.

WHO CAN CONDEMN US?

Who can condemn us?

'Who can condemn us, since Jesus is praying for us?' As I listen to young people speaking personally to me, I often wonder what can be the source of the feeling they have of being condemned, that burden of guilt which has nothing to do with sin.

Sin is a break with Jesus Christ. It means using others, making them victims of oneself.

Now all human tendencies, the best and the worst, are summed up in each individual, but that is not sin. Yes, every tendency without exception co-exists, to a greater or lesser extent, in every human being – urges to generosity or to murder, the desire to kill father or mother, brother or friend; all the affective tendencies; love and hatred; all in one single being.

When certain young people discover what they are and have no one to talk to, they conclude that they are little monsters, and they are driven to self-destruction, in extreme cases to suicide.

Who will condemn us? The norms of human societies? In every age, societies have spawned a process of self-defence, using guilt to force everyone into a mould with precise norms, the pattern of normality.

Before Christ, for example, little Israel, under constant threats to its existence, was anxious to ensure its continuity. So the barren woman was rejected and despised because, since she did not bear children, she had no place in the pattern of normality.

But for the Gospel, there is no 'normal' or 'abnormal', there are simply human beings in the image of God. The

Gospel knows only one norm – he who is supremely Man, Jesus Christ.

If, in spite of our inner contradictions, we set out again every morning towards Christ, it is not with any kind of normality in mind. It is with the ultimate goal in view, the goal beyond our hopes, that of becoming conformed to the very likeness of Jesus himself.

Who could condemn, since Christ is risen? He condemns no one; he never punishes.

Who could condemn? He is praying in us, offering us the liberation of forgiveness. We in our turn become liberators, never condemning anybody. Even in the struggle for human liberation, we are not going to be left in the rear. Perhaps every Christian is called to live as certain freedom-fighters have done, not hesitating to spend the whole night kneeling, in silence, before the reserved Sacrament?

Who could condemn? Even if our own heart condemns us, God is greater than our heart.

JOURNAL: 7 MARCH–24 OCTOBER 1973

7 March
Discussed the meaning of Lent with a young pastor, who is spending a few days in retreat here. Lent: forty days granted us in which to marvel at a love too great for words.

6 April
Today, can there be any other direction for the Christian than the way with a name hard to write: the way of holiness? I am afraid to call the young to follow it. Too many of their elders might well smother so dazzling a flame.

17 April
Conversation with two young men, standing beside the icon of the Virgin in the church. They have been preparing to become priests, but hesitate to take the final step. Every human being is full of inner contradictions, the present is a time of enormous changes, and the value of the ministry is frequently disputed: all of which makes them realise that being a 'witness' today means being a 'martyr', the original meaning of the word.

18 April

Wide awake at five this morning, I go down into the wood. From the back of her kennel, the dog sees me go by. I make signs so that, although she licks my hands as usual, she will not wake up the whole house by yelping. She understands my language. If only we too could understand the language of the birds flying away beneath the branches, disturbed in their morning chorus!

23 April

Easter Monday. It was no small effort, for all who had worked to prepare these last days' meeting, to welcome such a mass of people.

Reflected about the way we go forward together. Since the announcement of the Council of Youth, part of my charge has been to listen and sum up with others – not only with the intercontinental teams, but also spontaneously with one or another. In exceptional circumstances my service could also be to arbitrate, but that has never been necessary. We have never been brought to a standstill. That only goes to show how great is the vitality inspiring each and every one; during the last three years, the path has sometimes been steep.

6 May

The situation in the Middle East is getting worse. There is talk of a black May, after a black September. Some of the fedayin, condemned more and more by world opinion, grow increasingly desperate. What can we do for people who are slaughtering one another? This morning, during my weekly meeting with the people here, I dwelt on this topic. Afterwards, I discovered that there was an Arab Christian from Amman present, on his way home. He came to talk with me.

17 May

A dream: we are approaching harbour but, as we are about to berth, we find ourselves being driven back out to sea.

18 May

Week made heavy by a brother's illness. Christophe is at death's door. The doctors have discovered a brain tumour. At the hospital, between two periods of coma, I was able to tell him, 'Your mother is praying with you.' She died many years ago, but we often used to talk about her.

29 May

A German girl, on the point of leaving, remarks, 'When we return home, we shall be out in the world, while you all stay here.' But everyone takes the 'world' with them, wherever they are. It is with them in teeming crowds as well as in solitude, and even in dreams, when we consider ourselves far removed from everything by sleep.

9 June

To get from others what we want, in Christian circles – and elsewhere too – how often do we either play upon people's guilty consciences, or else make prophecies of doom?

12 June

A letter from Jacques in India. He writes about the encounter with Hinduism and Buddhism, which obliges us to leave our familiar world completely. Here in the West even Marxism and humanism, with which we try to have dialogue, are still secularised derivatives of Christianity.

17 June

Trinity Sunday. This morning Christophe died. I want to join my brothers, who also are suffering from this loss, but an hour alone is a comfort. Until the very end, I had hoped that he would be spared, even if as an invalid. In recent months, well before his accident, I had imagined him living among us as a 'staretz'.

20 June

Listen, listen, never force. My charge imposes a solitude, and I want to consent to it. If I could be conscious every day that this portion of solitude is reserved solely for His presence . . . Listen, never force. Understand with the heart, the mind will catch up later.

10 July

Once again, during a private conversation, I hear a familiar question: How can I be myself? How can I fulfil myself? Those questions preoccupy some people to the point of anguish.

I remember what Johan once said, talking of his encounter with Jesus: 'He does not say, be yourself; he says, be with me.' How right he is! Christ does not tell us, 'Find yourself' or 'Run after yourself'. He says, 'You, follow me.'

If 'being oneself' means dropping our masks, giving up conformist attitudes and conventions, who would disagree? That is not just good, it is vital.

On the other hand, a person is chasing illusions if, in the quest to be himself, his ego so asserts itself that it exists at the expense of other people's freedom, and swells up like a leech.

A person growing like this on the backs of others, at their expense, may not necessarily exclude God from his life. But although God is not rejected, he is far from being the essential.

When the Gospel asks people to be themselves and develop their gifts and talents a hundredfold, it is not in order to serve their own ends, it is to serve others.

In the Gospel, to be oneself means searching deeply until the irreplaceable gift given to each one of us is revealed. Through that special gift, unlike anyone else's, each person is brought to fulfilment in God.

So keep silence, withdraw into the desert, if only once in a lifetime, and discover that gift . . .

11 July

With so many people giving up the faith, there are Christians who console themselves with the thought that there will always be a 'small remnant'. But what then becomes of the vocation to be universal, to be a leaven of communion in the midst of humanity? Joy at being part of a 'small remnant' of the People of God can easily turn into the self-satisfaction of exclusive minorities.

12 July

Adrien's daily weather reports arouse enthusiasm. Perhaps he will be able to work as a meteorologist at Taizé, and persuade the meteorological service to set up a station equipped with the instruments he needs. That would certainly be the last thing we could ever have imagined having on the hill!

16 July

Yesterday evening, paused for a long time beside the oak tree at the bend in the path, looking at the sky. At ground level, the branches were rustling in a faint breeze. High above, the clouds were dancing in the light of the full moon, driven by squall after squall from west to east.

Back in my room again, sitting perched on the window-sill with my feet dangling above the porch roof, I could not tear my eyes away from the wind-blown clouds. The moon appeared and disappeared. Whenever it was veiled, the night became incandescent.

During the common prayer this morning, the conviction came that no burden would be too great. Everything seemed desirable. And now the day continues, bathed in that peaceful light, with the certainty of a presence.

Why are such moments of intensity so easily forgotten, as though they had never been? It is not a waste of time to note them down.

4 August

Long talk with Ivan Restrepo. He has just spent five years writing a doctoral thesis about Taizé. Only a Jesuit, and a South American one at that, would ever have had the courage to spend so long on such a job. I really cannot understand why Taizé is chosen as a thesis topic in universities. How many students have we already dissuaded? To understand what we are trying to live, the perspective of time is necessary, even for ourselves. As far as Ivan is concerned, those who have read his thesis say it is of real value.

8 August

There are people who always want to be in at the start. If they have not been involved in the initial stages of a creation, they do not care to be associated with it. Do they not understand that there is no more creativity present at the beginnings of a venture than later on? Creativity is sometimes expressed more in continuity and duration. Otherwise all that remains is the short-lived adventure, but when the dazzling fireworks have burned out, we are left in the dark.

For us here at Taizé, creativity is as manifest in the last twelve years as it was in the first ones.

4 September

Relived intensely an evening in the summer of 1942, when I was still on my own in Taizé. I was sitting writing at a small table. I knew that I was in danger because of the political refugees I was sheltering in the house. The risk that I would be arrested was considerable. Members of the civilian police force had repeatedly made raids and questioned me. That evening, with fear in the pit of my stomach, a prayer took hold of me. I said it to God without really understanding what I was saying: 'Take my life if you think fit, but let what has begun here continue.' Yet what had been begun in those two years? Principally a welcoming house and prayer in solitude.

5 September

Long talk with a small group of those who take a large share in the responsibility of making people welcome here. We discuss the Council of Youth now in preparation.

In the Northern hemisphere at present we are confronted with a breakdown of 'moral memory'. One expression of this lies in the rejection of every form of faithfulness. Everything has to be lived in the present moment.

This loss of 'moral memory' was becoming a vital question for our ecumenical vocation in Taizé, and then the answer appeared: to prepare a Council of Youth. The very idea of taking four and a half years together, in order to prepare ourselves for something which itself will last for years, is a challenge.

The Council of Youth will be no ordinary adventure. It will not be a congress or forum, a platform for current ideas. To have chosen to call it a Council means that it is an adventure lived in the Body of Christ, his Church – that irreplaceable communion set in the midst of a suffering, searching world, a world that without realising it aspires after new birth.

16 September

Some people jealously treasure in their hearts a piece of broken glass. It hurts them whenever they like, and with it they also tend to wound those around them.

20 September

Children! Those who often come and kneel beside me in church during the common prayer . . . What they discover will remain with them forever. So never deprive a child of that current of contemplation which will carry him throughout his life.

21 September

Here again, at the round table with its decayed pine-wood top. The very sight of the wood awakens dreams of childhood in the Juras. In every poor villager's home, the pine-wood surfaces shone brightly, polished with much rubbing of cloths.

An hour as rounded as the table, everything coming together. No discontinuity between the hours of my youth and those of today. They tend rather to nourish one another.

Sitting on the little stool, also of pine wood, I take up my pen once more, like a craftsman called to labour on and on.

25 September
Conversation with a scientist. A high price must be paid for great gifts of intelligence, or for genius. The other sides have to be accepted as well, and they are on a par with the abilities.

1 October
Visit from the Archbishop of Canterbury. Talking to the young people here, he says: 'The Council of Youth will not be one more organisation, or a new movement. Through it, many young people will help the Church, all over the world, to become a Church able to forget herself, laying aside all pride, all power, all wealth.'

15 October
Certain tensions in the Council of Youth arise from persons rather than ideas. Far from halting us, they help us to go forward. What will count in the end will be the communion continually rediscovered. All the rest will pass, without leaving much trace.

As for our community, its vocation to live an anticipation of communion in the Church is even more precise than we had ever imagined. We are asked to keep on striving after a certain sense of perspective and inner silence, and to go on taking risks.

45

23 October

Birthday lunch for Nicholas. We invited Cristobal. We talk about the flooding in southern Spain. Cristobal recalls how, when he was ten, he saw a river burst its banks and a torrent of water and mud come crashing down. Before his very eyes, the house of his best friend, Eduardo, was destroyed. As the walls collapsed he saw Eduardo's body being swept away by the waters. During the whole of the next week, every day he spent time in the local church, before the Sacrament. He wrestled with God, asking why Eduardo was gone. After eight days he found peace. He had told God, 'You are all I have.' At that point, Cristobal began to cry; he wept for a long, long time. We decided to leave the dessert for another time and Cristobal promised, 'I will come and sing flamencos.' At table tonight, tirelessly, Cristobal sang.

24 October

Gather everything that happens, trivialities included, without reservation, regret or nostalgia, in inexhaustible wonder.

Set out, forward, one step at a time, from doubt towards faith, not worrying about the impossible ahead. Light fire, even with the thorns that tear you.

FROM DOUBT TOWARDS BELIEVING

From doubt towards believing

No one is built naturally for living the radicalism of the Gospel. In every person the yes and the no are super-imposed.

Yet it is through giving himself totally that a person grows. If he risks his whole life, that becomes the preparation for events beyond his wildest hopes. Situations of standstill, discouragement or fierce struggle, far from demolishing, build him up. The ways through darkness are travelled stage by stage, the solitude of the long, dim nights, with human thirsts unquenched ... bitterness, that gangrene of the heart ... storms ... all the fears that crouch at life's turning-points ...

What if the ground is overgrown with thorns, scrub-wood and briars? With thorns, Christ lights a fire. Are there still roots of bitterness, is love still impossible? That goes to feed the fire. Weakness becomes a crucible where the yes is made and re-made and made new day after day. What most threatens man is transformed into a means of lightening his heaviness.

The moment comes when we receive what we no longer even expected. What we had never dared to hope for arises. A gleam of Christ in us. Others see it shining, although we are unaware of it. Nothing is to be gained by knowing what light we reflect; many people already reflect God's brightness without knowing it, perhaps even without daring to believe it.

For those who risk their whole lives, no road ever comes to a dead end.

We think we have abandoned Christ, but he does not abandon us.

We think that we have forgotten him, yet he was there.

And we set out once more, we begin all over again, he is present.

That is the unexpected; that is what we had not dared hope for.

Confronted with the radicalism of the Gospel and the risks it implies, many people take fright. Doubt remains. Some do not know if they are still believers or not.

It is never Christ who is absent or far away from man, it is man who is distracted, far off or indifferent. Christ's existence is independent of man, he is not confined to the subjective feelings we may or may not have of him.

If we are more aware of doubt now than in the past, this is the result of our greater readiness to accept that pockets of incredulity remain in us.

In the past, 'I believe', 'Credo', sprang more easily to the lips; today, many prefer to tell God first 'I love you' and then, much later on, 'I believe'.

More than a century ago, at a moment when Christians were for the first time asking such questions about doubt and faith, Dostoyevsky wrote from his Siberian prison: 'I am a child of disbelief and doubt, to this very hour and even, I am sure, to my last breath. How great are the sufferings I have had to endure from this thirst to believe, which only grows stronger in my soul with the growth in me of arguments to the contrary.' Yet Dostoyevsky goes on to insist that in his eyes, 'There is nothing more beautiful, more profound, more congenial, more reasonable, more virile, more perfect than Christ and not only is there nothing, but with a jealous love I say that there can be nothing. Still more, if someone were to demonstrate to me that Christ is outside of truth, and that truth really lies outside of Christ, I would rather stay with Christ than with truth.'

When Dostoyevsky suggests that the non-believer

coexists in him with the believer, the no with the yes, his passionate love for Christ still remains undiminished. Child of doubt and disbelief, he nonetheless hears Christ's 'Do you love me?' and returns, day after day, to the journey from doubt towards believing.

JOURNAL: 26 OCTOBER 1973–6 APRIL 1974

26 October
Situations sometimes arise in which a young couple can see no other way of maintaining their unity than by making a clean break with father and mother. But a break of that kind brings only temporary peace, since for basic stability it is so essential to have father and mother integrated in oneself.

Never allow oneself to have guilt feelings arising out of the frustration of a father who, without realising it, had a passion for his daughter, or a mother over-attached to her son. Those parental attitudes are as old as the hills. Parents often have no control over their possessive love, the result of inner distress. It is important to understand them as best one can, and above all not to imprison them by our condemnation.

17 November
In Paris, to see Cardinal Silva of Santiago in Chile, who is on a brief visit to France. It took me a few seconds to recognise him, his face had grown gaunt and deeply furrowed. But the eyes remained unchanged.

It is certain that people are suffering in other countries too, but the tragedy of Chile brands many, and leaves them deeply troubled. It must be said that one day we were given the possibility of intervening from Taizé to save a human life, that of Luis Corvalan, the General Secretary of the Chilean Communist Party ... In that precise instance, I received clear proof of the courage of Pope Paul VI.

18 November
During a meeting in the church, Cristobal told all the young people here: 'We have to pass through the Garden of Olives, to know what it means to be abandoned by others, seemingly even by God, so as to reach the point where we can abandon ourselves in God. I am drawing near to that garden, I am still at the gate, not daring to enter but knowing that I must, if I want to accompany Christ, wait with him for Easter to come, and pass on to new life.'

2 December
Yesterday, in the waiting room at Mâcon railway station, we encounter three immigrant workers from Algeria. We begin to talk. Two of them have small children. Once a year they go to spend a few weeks with their families in North Africa. They make no embittered remarks as they tell of their difficulties at work, or when they look for lodgings. We are indebted to them for part of the development of Europe, and for the rise in our standard of living. Yet very many Europeans continue to treat them as outcasts.

4 December
For the last few days nothing more could be done for my mother; she could no longer take nourishment. This morning she was eager to calm everyone, and to Ghislain she said, 'Life is beautiful,' adding, 'We should always be glad.' This afternoon she murmured once more, 'Life is beautiful,' then repeated several times, 'Jésus ... c'est

beau.' Those were her last words. At eight this evening, while we were in church for the common prayer, she entered Christ's eternity. She passed away gently, her breath simply slowing to a halt.

A few years ago, after her first heart attack, as soon as she could speak again she uttered these words, 'I have no fear of dying, I know in whom I believe ... but I love life.'

15 December

Paris. During Mass at St Sulpice, the priest preaches on the meaning of community. In every community, there must be one person who sees that the whole body does not settle down in self-satisfaction, but opens more and more towards the universal.

So when you are ashamed of not being capable of fulfilling your charge, when you sometimes long to tear off the copper cross you wear over your prayer robe, remember that moment: 'In every community, there must be one person ...'

16 December

No fears for the salvation of humanity. God is love. For those who know it, fullness lies there. And as for all those who have never known anything of God, it was to visit them that Jesus descended 'to the lower regions' on Holy Saturday. He went down to every human being who had died before him. And now, every moment, in the same way he continues to visit all who do not know him ...

1 January 1974

This year, 1974, is perhaps the year for us to abandon everything in God; the burden is so excessive and the means are so limited. What if this year we were to let the Holy Spirit turn us into people of overflowing fullness? Without an overflowing heart, without a grasp of situations, everything shrinks, our vision of people and events becomes increasingly narrow.

3 January

Letter from a student: 'I left for Taizé on my own, hesitant about taking a step which would commit me further in the footsteps of Christ. Now I measure, or more precisely I sense, how far I have come in nine days spent on the hill. I expressed my attachment to Jesus Christ struggling to save all men. In the fatigue of a sleepless night I lived with Jesus Christ struggling in the Garden. During the common prayer every day, sitting back on my heels, as I looked at you brothers I thought, God really does call us to madness, to such a life at the same time so far from and so close to the world.

'I am studying economics. For the last eighteen months I have been faced with concrete problems of violence, psychological as to the absurdity of our subject-matter, physical as regards the police or extremist right-wing groups, or even the apathy of the great mass of students. Last summer I opted to become a militant for revolution, and the more I struggle, the more festival quickens me.

'If tomorrow I have to give my life, I know that elsewhere others have done so before me.'

11 January

For my brothers gathered in the little village church, I comment on a story in the Old Testament.

One day in the village called Zarephath, at a time of serious famine, an old woman sees Elijah, the man of God, come into her house. There is very little left in her ooil-jar and her flour-bin. But she does not hesitate to use it all to make three cakes, saying: 'Afterwards, we shall have nothing but death to look forward to.' She pushes her trust to the utmost limits, at which point, in a flash, God intervenes. The flour and the oil will never give out.

This year, with the opening of the Council of Youth approaching, there is not much flour in our sacks, and very little oil in our jars. But with this little, abundance is offered, unfailingly.

Committed to venture into the unknown for Christ, we can tell him already: I took you at your word, I regret nothing, if I had to begin all over again, I would take the same path.

Today as in the past, our community is continually roused to new efforts by the 'Church's torment' – the expression is from one of my brothers.

We are called to be part of a double movement: on the one hand, the renewal from within, untiringly, of all that can be renewed in the People of God; and on the other hand, daring to place ourselves in the front lines.

In the last ten years there has been much reawakening in the People of God throughout the world. Everywhere conformist habits are changing into personal adherence.

The march is slow, but none the less sure. Any attempt to hasten it is sure to arouse panic.

It involves making the values of popular belief our own and giving them new life from within, entering into the very heart of the masses so as to share their aspirations, hopes and distress.

Passion for communion in the Body of Christ, his Church, entitles no one to ride roughshod over the People of God in its slow progress. Anyone who would plunge the great mass of Christians into hopelessness in that way would be heartless. Very often it is child-like faith which has been passed on to them. Is anybody entitled to tie a stone around the neck of the simplest member of God's people, and so to wound the Body of Christ himself?

There are those sturdy enough to stand at the forefront of the Church's life; they take the risks and prepare the ways forward. Already, all over the world, Christians are becoming brothers and sisters of non-believers; that is one of the clear signs of our time. Christians everywhere are becoming more and more aware that they are part of the whole human community, and are called to be leaven of unity in a secularised world.

Keep within the body of the whole People of God, stay in the Church's front lines: there is no contradiction in those two aims.

Till my very last breath, I will use all the strength of my conviction to urge the greatest possible number of people to follow those paths.

6 February

In the United States with Robert and Thomas. Delight at discovering San Francisco. This is the second invitation from the bishops of the Anglican Communion, this time to speak about the Holy Spirit.

At present, when there is a revival of the Spirit, how can gifts and charisms be lived to complement one another, so that they do not exclude each other?

Among all the young people I listen to at Taizé, those known as charismatics are often a real refreshment. But I feel obliged to say: if I try to understand what the Spirit is saying to the Church through you, try in your turn to understand what the Spirit is saying through those who have other points of view – unselfish political concern, for example. Listen and understand.

At the same time I tell others: The charismatics experience a release in their very depths, a heightened sensitivity, allowing them to express freely a whole range of human possibilities which have hitherto remained latent.

2 March

After the lowering skies of late February, and then yesterday's squalls, today the wind has thinned the clouds, here and there dispersing the dark masses. All morning long, a *tachiste* painting kept appearing, then melting away. Look with new eyes, and learn to love even the subtle lighting of these last few days.

3 March

Ivan Restrepo writes to announce the death of Diego, one of his young Jesuit brothers. I knew him. When he was studying in Lyon, before he returned to Colombia, he used to come to Taizé. He died of cancer, in the space of a few weeks. Living in an iron lung, he could only communicate by writing notes. On the morning of 13 February he wrote, 'Is it serious?' Ivan, who was close by, did not hide the truth. Later that morning he wrote, 'Roger's book.' They brought it. A few minutes later he wrote, 'If I die, put these words on my grave: May your festival never end.' He fell asleep, and died soon after.

Diego's last wish will bear me along until my race reaches its goal.

4 March
Letter from a Catholic bishop who recently spent a few days with us:

'In Taizé, everything is already full of high expectancy for the Council of Youth. You feel yourself caught up by a rushing wind of the Spirit that shakes the Church to its very foundations, not trying to destroy, but eager to break down walls in order to prepare it to welcome great multitudes searching for a hope capable of giving life to the world, and of inspiring the younger generations to build a world of justice and fraternity, signs of the Kingdom to come. It is only natural that this expectancy is mingled with anxiety; it involves abandoning oneself to the Spirit. With him there is no telling where things will end; he upsets all human reckoning. I have a strong feeling that the Council of Youth, in spite of all the trials, the resistances, the inevitable gaps and failures, will be a new step forward for the Church and for all mankind. That hope may seem ridiculous and out of all proportion to staid, realistic Christians, but the parable of the mustard seed, and the parable of the little carpenter who becomes the risen Lord, is a utopia that never fails to come into being despite all predictions to the contrary. Pentecost is not over yet.'

13 March
Thought several times recently of what should have been my first book. I am sorry now that I destroyed the manuscript, as I destroy all my old papers. That manuscript

would have told me something about the choices I made when I was young.

If I had published *Evolution of a Puritan Boyhood* at the time I wrote it, when I was twenty, my life would probably have taken another turn. Why was it quite impossible for me to rewrite the end of the book in the way that Jean Paulhan, director of the *Nouvelle Revue Française*, suggested? He would have published it if I had. Why was I so convinced that my manuscript formed a whole as it stood, and therefore could not be modified? It was the outcome of the combat and discoveries of my early youth.

25 March
A priest who tries to be priest and layman at the same time denies the laity its own specific ministry – he wants to be everything at once.

29 March
Two young refugees from Chile, recently in Taizé, said, 'Here you are called to sow and sow again, without concerning yourselves about the harvest.'

5 April
Over the last few years, have spoken to so many young men who have given up the idea of becoming priests. They are afraid of finding no community, and so of being plunged into a solitude more exposed than ever before. I ask myself whether the time has not come to ordain married men?

For over a thousand years, in the Catholic Church celibacy and priesthood have gone together, and I know what this centuries-old tradition signifies. Still, the sharp drop in priestly and pastoral vocations poses a question.

The present upheavals in the Church have their roots in the enormous transformations which our human societies are undergoing. It is not true that God is punishing his Church: he is carrying her forward more visibly than ever before. He is not creating a vacuum. Already, at the same time as the life-blood of vocations is being lost, he offers a means of healing: the ministry in which every baptised member of the laity shares is being developed in new, unforeseen ways.

Certainly, local communities animated by courageous lay people will go far. But can they do without somebody to bring them all together and to preside at the Eucharist, the source and fulfilment of all communion? Surely, when married men demonstrate the obvious ability to become such gatherers and animators, does not a question arise demanding an answer? Can we go on depriving local communities of such shepherds?

Admittedly, the experience of some Protestant pastors' families can make us wonder. There are children who live trapped in 'minister's family' situations. But on the other hand, there are all those wives devotedly assisting their husbands in their ministry, not to mention the host of children of Orthodox priests or Protestant pastors, active in the workaday world, who ensure the living continuity of Christ, because their childhood was nourished by the essence of their father's ministry.

Has the time come for the Catholic Church to confer the priesthood on married men? I raise the question with the authority given by the fact that I came to Taizé and called others to choose to live a whole lifetime committed to celibacy in community. That has shown me the quality of mystic communion which celibacy brings.

If we made all the commitments to life in community, except for celibacy, we would never realise how utterly men can be consumed with passion for communion in the Body of Christ.

6 April
Anyone who lives for himself alone is more dead than alive. If the aim of living is merely to last as long as possible, existence has no meaning. Whoever consents to lose his life hears a call beyond himself.

LOVED WITH ETERNITY'S LOVE

Loved with Eternity's love

'Do you love me?' is Jesus' final question to Peter. Peter was saddened and appalled: three times over he had denied Jesus before his torture on a cross. Now the risen Lord stands before him. But Jesus does not condemn him for his denial! He does not adopt an attitude of strength. He does nothing to tighten that noose of bad conscience already round Peter's neck. Christ's compassion is the heart of his humanity; he too, during his earthly life, passed through ways of darkness.

To Peter, Christ says only these few words: Do you love me? And Peter replies: Lord, you know I love you. A second time, Jesus asks: Do you love me? Again Peter answers: But you know I love you! A third time, Jesus insists: Do you love me more than the others do? And Peter is troubled: Lord, you know everything; you know how I love you!

Since that day, Christ keeps on tirelessly asking every human being: Do you love me?

There are days when we refuse to listen; the question becomes intolerable. It is unbearable for any who have never experienced human love, for those who feel totally forsaken, who experience nothing but the wound dealt to their childhood innocence. It is unbearable for all of us, when it uncovers within us the place of solitude no human intimacy can ever fill, that place of solitude where God is waiting for us. And when our revolt is at its height, the question rings like a condemnation, so true it is that nobody can love by sheer will-power.

Do we realise fully enough that Christ never obliges anyone to love him? But he, the living Christ, is standing at each one's side, poor and humble. He is there, even in our sorriest moments – when our life is at its most vulnerable. His love is a presence, not for a fleeting moment, but for ever. It is Eternity's love, opening a way of becoming, beyond ourselves. Without that elsewhere, without that way of becoming lying beyond us, we have no hope . . . and the urge to advance fades away.

Confronted with Eternity's endless loving, we sense that our real response cannot be temporary, just for a while, before we resume the old life once more. Neither can our response be a mere effort of will. This would break certain people. Rather it means surrendering ourselves.

To come before him, with words or without, is to respond in poverty and find where our hearts can rest. This is the secret impulse, impetus enough for a whole lifetime, the risk of the Gospel. 'Although sometimes I cannot tell whether I love you or not, you, Christ, know everything, you know that I love you.'

Great happiness is offered to all who take the risks of such love, not stopping to calculate all the consequences. Once we seek happiness as an end in itself, we eventually see that happiness fade – the more passionately we try to hold on to it, the farther it flees.

Ardent seeker of Eternity's unending love, whoever you are, do you want to find your heart's rest? Through your very wound, he opens the gate to fullness – the praise of his love. Surrender yourself, give yourself. There lies healing for wounds, and not for yours alone; already, in him, we are healed by one another.

JOURNAL: 8 APRIL–30 AUGUST 1974

8 April

Shall be in London tomorrow. This is only the second time the Templeton Prize is being awarded. When I learned that I had been chosen, I thought of Mother Teresa receiving it last year, and of my brothers working with her among the dying in Calcutta.

Accept this award for reconciliation in simplicity of heart, solely as a confirmation offered by other believers – Buddhists, Hindus, Muslims, Jews and Christians – to the believer you try to be, day after day.

The large sum of money attached to the award will not be for the community. We have always refused gifts, living by our work alone, without any capital reserves. Neither can I accept it to offer better hospitality to people coming to Taizé, even though our funds have given out for the time being.

I and others have asked the young people staying on the hill in recent weeks to whom the money should go. It will be given to young people, particularly in the Southern parts of the world, who are committed to ways of struggle and contemplation, striving to be untiring seekers of communion. Part of it will go to young people in the British Isles who are working to provide a welcome to immigrants from Africa and Asia, and to others struggling for reconciliation in Northern Ireland.

10 April
More often than ever before people ask me, 'What is the most important thing in your life?'

Unhesitatingly I reply: our common prayer, and in it, the periods of silence.

Then, immediately after that, the best thing in my life: when I am talking with someone alone, to perceive the whole human being, the drama they can scarcely bear to reveal, the knot of a permanent failure or break in the inner life; but also the unique gifts through which the life of God in them is able to bring everything to fulfilment.

Far from being disconcerted when they reveal to me what they can hardly bear to put into words, I try to comprehend them as a whole person, by means of a few words or attitudes rather than by lengthy attempts at explanation.

Intuition comes to the aid of understanding, most fully itself when called upon to grasp all that the other person is going through. Sensitivity, sharpened with the years, has a part to play as well. Nowadays my time is far more limited than it used to be, so I am all the more alert to grasp instantly what really is at stake.

It is not enough simply to share those hidden things that have caused a person's wounds. It is even more vital to search for that special gift of God, the pivot of their whole existence. Once this gift (or gifts) has been brought to light, all roads are open.

No dwelling on the knots, tragedies, failures and conflicting forces; hundreds of contradictory reasons for them can always be found. Move on as quickly as possible to the essential: uncovering the unique gift, the talents entrusted to every human being, intended not to lie buried but to be brought to full life in God.

The best thing in my life? I could go on for ever: those rare occasions when I suddenly find myself free to drop everything and go out ... walking for hours

and conversing in the streets of some great city ...
sharing a meal with guests round a table ... the sight
of a brother coming into my room, and admiring in his
transparency his honesty with himself, his refusal to be
drawn into labyrinths ...

11 April

What will today bring for the young man who waited
yesterday in the church until everyone else had gone,
so as to be the last to speak to me? A little way off, his
wife was looking on. Through what he said, I sensed
the rupture deep within him which today leads him to
one break after another. What will his future be? I am
confident. What he had alwayys kept bottled up somehow
exploded; he was able to express himself at last. Slowly
everything will fall into place. I expect a letter from
him.

What will today bring for F.? I discovered him yesterday too. He is about to leave for Mexico, as a political
exile. 'Do your parents know what is happening?' I
asked. 'No, they are simple people, they could never
understand. It would kill my mother.' He does not com-
plain. He only came to greet me and receive the blessing
of Christ. He explains that this moment will take the
place of saying farewell to his elderly parents.

16 April

Easter Week. One thing which can already be clearly
sensed about the Council of Youth is that it will not be
able to make do with people who only commit themselves
halfway; it can only use men and women who, step by
step, commit themselves totally.

We will never proselytise, neither for the Council of
Youth itself, nor for anybody in the world. We are not
setting ourselves free from cold, authoritarian, doc-
trinaire systems, only to go headlong into other systems
which are bound to imprison, however tempting they
may appear.

18 April
So many people hide behind their own words! It sometimes happens that those who are least committed to
Christ and to justice succeed in disguising their lack of
commitment by professing with their lips irrefutable
ideals or doctrines.

26 April
Have often thought about the need to simplify still further our *Rule of Taizé*, beginning with the title. It is not
at all a rule in the normal sense. It tries to point out a
simple path for living a parable of communion.

6 May
The woodpecker will be heard tapping no more. His
favourite haunt, the dead catalpa tree, has been cut down
and burned. Its ashes will be used for glazing in the pot-
tery. A tree falls! I still remember the old chestnut tree
which had to be cut down one day after lightning had
split it in two. Here on our hill, the rock is close to the
surface and the soil is not good. So every tree counts.

7 May
Late last evening, four Africans arrived. Two of them are
exiles from their own country. I stirred up the fire in my
room, made them welcome and listened to what they had
to say. One told how his parents were killed, simply because they belonged to a certain tribe. In this corner of
Burgundy, they now have a new family.

8 May
Letter from a young Portuguese poet: 'On 25 April, the
poorest people in Europe showed that it is possible to
achieve a revolution without violence. It is a date to remember. A flame of hope is burning in our land. You
could say that a child has been born, without too much

suffering. At the moment, we do not know what colour its eyes will be, but its first cries were so wonderful that a whole people woke up for joy. Pray that this newborn hope will grow and flourish. In the past few days I have been longing to send you a telegram, with these simple words: come and see.'

10 May
It would be easy to inform the press of the difficulties we encounter with certain men at the head of Church institutions. We would win immediate sympathy, but it would be too easy; we would be working against the communion of the Body of Christ. It is an exercise in self-restraint to keep silent at such times. Try to understand those who oppose and perhaps one day, unexpectedly, a person-to-person talk will take place and everything will suddenly become clear.

11 May
All through Christian history, great renewals have happened at times when there was burning love for the Word of God.

That fire dies down as soon as the Scriptures are frozen into a system, hardening into doctrines as cold as ice. People today are so aware of this that there is a certain instinctive mistrust of all 'ex cathedra' teaching, even when it is firmly rooted in Scripture. They prefer to prove God by living him rather than by reasoning. In modern eyes, practice comes before teaching. A young theologian told me the same thing in his own way: 'orthopraxis before orthodoxy'.

17 May
In the *Rule of Taizé* obedience is never mentioned. When I was writing it, almost twenty-five years ago, I was aware that great changes were taking place in human consciousness. Whatever their motivation, people today try

to use to the full the unique gifts they have received. They see obedience as inhibiting.

Yet no community can long survive, steadily moving ahead over mountains and valleys, unless it accepts in its very centre the pastoral service of one person, just as no cell in a human body can remain alive without a central nucleus. This person's principal service is to lead each to discover his own gift, and freely contribute it to the common creation.

7 June

Increasingly convinced, in recent years, of the existence of a whole realm of darkness, imponderable but active. Visible in encounters when a disguised need to dominate arises, or a slight breeze of inquisition begins to blow. The believer is the favourite victim, being more exposed and defenceless.

This conviction goes contrary to current popular opinion that the tempter does not really exist. That we have got rid of the devil with his cloven hoofs and his tail, as one of the terrors of the past, is just as well. But who could forget that Christ faced the tempter forty days and nights?

12 June

Rest your heart in God, let yourself float on the safe waters, loving life as it comes, with all the rough weather it may bring. Give, without counting how many years are left, not wworried about surviving as long as possible.

18 June

A few days away from home, and I miss it already. It was just the same when I was a child. The first days spent away from home were holidays with my father's mother. I used to set off with incomparable delight. Once there, I would spend hours listening to her. Dressed in black, erect and motionless, she used to talk about the tremendous grief of her childhood, how her mother had declined and died in the space of three weeks, made blind by constant weeping over the family's troubles.

After only a few days, I would be bored. I used to long for home, to see the familiar house and the trees. My aunt, who lived with my grandmother, must have played a major part in that boredom. She used to spend all her time re-educating me. 'You don't put your fingers on the sharp edge of the knife. You keep your hands on the edge of the table, not too far forward. You don't put your hands on your knees.' I felt that my aunt was criticising my parents. She considered my father much too simple in his tastes, and that my mother attached more importance to music than to her nine children. Everyone dreaded that aunt's remarks, so it was always the youngest who was sent to spend holidays with her!

2 July
At the end of next month, the Council of Youth will open. With all the suggestions received, it had seemed certain that by now we would see clearly enough how to live the opening. Not at all. This feeling of a vacuum is unexpected, hardly forseeable, but by no means a real trial. Confidence is not shaken. On 30 August, we shall set out on the new stage with the little we have understood, and nothing more. Then the void will be filled.

Why this confidence? The Council of Youth is so little our affair, so much Christ's. We shall simply be eyewitnesses, astonished and sometimes amazed. All that is authentic and vast in what we live must come from him. There are voids which only stimulate a greater certainty.

13 July
There are people who are dying of a thirst for domination and who, to maintain their existence, attempt to annihilate others by word or look. When, in their

confusion, they employ analytical notions only half-understood, they are considered authorities; they learn how to act the great expert and wreak their havoc. Never harden yourself when faced with destructive individuals. But never join them in that prison of their own choosing.

20 July

Meeting with a group of young Asians, North Americans, Africans, Latin Americans and Europeans, to discuss the opening of the Council of Youth. They think that one expression of this opening will be a letter addressed to the People of God, to communicate the aspirations burning in the hearts of the young. They have begun to work on it. I for my part will try to write another letter designed to point out a few essential directions by which a whole life can be fashioned. A kind of little 'rule of life' to accompany people through the years. It might be called 'A life we never dared hope for.'

25 July

For years we have been searching for reciprocity between the Northern and Southern hemispheres, but the gap shows no signs of being filled in. Everywhere, condemnation and intransigence. There as here, young people are generous in the extreme. But this generation is doubly victim: because of a divorce between separated Christians, and an economic system in which some are anaesthetised by poverty, and others by the uncontrolled urge to consume.

30 August 1974

The day has come, this opening day of the Council of Youth, the day when we all long to say: open yourself to understand each person fully, each woman and man, made of the same stuff as you and who, like you, searches, struggles, creates, prays.

The day has come after long waiting, in common searching, with all the tensions which that involves. And what has finally prevailed has been trusting love.

On 20 August 1940, when I arrived in this human wasteland, there was nothing to suggest these days when forty thousand young people would be gathered together at Taizé. And all those far away as well, those very dear to us who are reduced to silence, imprisoned, suffering because of the Gospel and their struggle for justice and freedom.

With all of them, with people from every part of the world, we are being called to a life that exceeds all our hopes.

A LIFE WE NEVER DARED
HOPE FOR

A life we never dared hope for

I know you want to fashion your life in communion with Christ who is love, so I have written this letter for you. You will feel freer to move from one provisional stage to the next, if you rely throughout your life on a small number of essential values – a few simple truths.

Together with the whole people of God, with people from all over the world, you are invited to live a life exceeding all your hopes. On your own, how could you ever experience the radiance of God's presence?

God is too dazzling to be looked upon. He is a God who blinds our sight. It is Christ who channels this consuming fire, and allows God to shine through without dazzling us.

Christ is present, close to each one of us, whether we know him or not. He is so bound up with us that he lives within us, even when we are unaware of him. He is there in secret, a fire burning in the heart, a light in the darkness.

But Christ is also someone other than yourself. He is alive; he stands beyond, ahead of you.

Here is his secret: he loved you first.

That is the meaning of your life: to be loved for ever, loved to all eternity, so that you, in turn, will dare to die for love. Without love, what is the point of living?

From now on, in prayer or in struggle, only one thing is disastrous, the loss of love. Without love, what is the good of believing, or even of giving your body to the flames?

Do you see? Contemplation and struggle arise from the very same source, Christ who is love.

If you pray, it is out of love. If you struggle to restore dignity to the exploited, that too is for love.

Will you agree to set out on this road? At the risk of losing your life for love, will you live Christ for others?

With people all over the world
On our own, what can we do to give the voiceless their say, and to promote a society without class?

With the whole people of God, collectively, it is possible to light a fire on the earth.

One of Christ's questions hits home. When that poor person was hungry, did you recognise me in him? Where were you when I was sharing the life of the utterly destitute? Have you been the oppressor of even one single human being? When I said 'Woe to the rich' – rich in money, or rich in dogmatic certainties – did you prefer the illusions of wealth?

Your struggle cannot be lived out in ideas that fly from pillar to post and never become reality.

Break the oppressions of the poor and the exploited, and to your astonishment you will see signs of resurrection springing up, here and now.

Share all you have for greater justice. Make no one your victim. Brother to all, a universal brother, run to whoever is despised and rejected.

'Love those who hate you. Pray for those who wrong you.' In hatred, how could you reflect anything of Christ? 'Love your neighbour as yourself.' If you hated yourself, what damage that would do!

But as your life has been filled to overflowing, you try to understand everything in others.

The closer you come to communion, the more efforts the tempter will make. To be free of him, sing Christ until you are joyful and serene.

Tensions can be creative. But when your relationship with someone has deteriorated into seething inner contradictions and non-communication, remember that beyond the desert something else lies waiting.

We judge other people by what we are ourselves, by our own hearts. Remember only the best you have found in others. With words of liberation on your lips, not a mouthful of condemnation, do not waste your energy looking at the speck in your brother's eye.

If you suffer unfair criticism for the sake of Christ, dance and forgive as God has forgiven. You will find that you are free, free beyond compare.

In any disagreement, what is the point of trying to find out who was right and who was wrong?

Have nothing to do with clever diplomacy; aim at transparency of heart; never manipulate another's conscience, using his anxiety as a lever to force him into your scheme of things.

In every domain, when things are too easy creativity is low. Poverty of means leads to living intensely, in the joy of the present moment. But joy vanishes if poverty of means leads to austerity or to judging others.

Poverty of means gives birth to a sense of the universal. And the festival begins once more. The festival will never end.

If festival disappeared from mankind . . . If we were to wake up, one fine morning, in a society replete but emptied of all spontaneity . . . If praying became mere words, so secularised that it lost all sense of mystery, leaving no room for the prayer of gesture and posture, for poetry, for emotion or for intuition . . . If we were to lose childlike trust in the Eucharist and the Word of God . . . If, on our grey days, we were to demolish all we had grasped on days of light . . . If we were to decline the joy offered by Him who eight times over declares 'Happy' (Matt. 5).

If festival disappears from the Body of Christ, if the Church is a place of retrenchment and not of universal comprehension, in all the world where could we find a place of friendship for the whole of mankind?

We are ourselves only in God's presence
If you feel no sense of God's presence within you when you pray, why worry? There is no precise dividing-line

between emptiness and fullness, any more than between doubt and faith, or fear and love.

The essential is always concealed from your own eyes. But that only makes you more eager than ever to progress towards the one reality. Then, gradually, it becomes possible to sense something of the depth and the breadth of a love beyond all comprehension. At that point you touch the gates of contemplation, and there you draw the energy you need for new beginnings, for daring commitments.

Discovering what kind of person you are, with nobody there to understand you, can provoke a sense of shame at being alive, strong enough to lead to self-destruction. At times it makes you feel that you are living under sentence. But, for the Gospel, there is neither 'normal' nor 'abnormal', only human beings, made in the image of God. Then who could condemn? Jesus prays in you. He offers the liberation of forgiveness to all who live in poverty of heart, so that they, in their turn, may become liberators of others.

In every single one of us there is a place of solitude no human relationship can fill, not even the deepest love between two individuals. Anyone who does not accept this solitude sooner or later revolts against other people, and against God himself.

And yet you are never alone. Let yourself be plumbed to the depths, and you will realise that everyone is created for a presence. There, in your heart of hearts, in that place where no two people are alike, Christ is waiting for you. And there the unexpected happens.

In a flash, the love of God, the Holy Spirit, streaks through each one of us like lightning in our night. The risen Christ takes hold of you, and he takes over. He takes upon himself everything that is unbearable. It is only later, sometimes much later, that you realise: Christ came, he gave his overflowing life.

The moment your eyes are opened you will say, 'My heart was burning within me as he spoke.'

Christ does not destroy flesh and blood. In communion with him there is no room for alienation. He does not break what is in us. He has not come to destroy, but to fulfil. When you listen, in the silence of your heart, he transfigures all that troubles you most. When you are shrouded in what you cannot understand, when darkness gathers, his love is a flame. You need only fix your gaze on that lamp burning in the darkness, till day begins to dawn and the sun rises in your heart.

Happy are they who die for love
Never a pause, O Christ, in your persistent questioning: 'Who do you say that I am?'

You are the one who loves me into endless life.

You open up the way of risk. You go ahead of me along the way of holiness, where happy are they who die of love, where the ultimate response is martyrdom.

Day by day you transfigure the 'No' in me into 'Yes'. You ask me, not for a few scraps, but for the whole of my existence.

You are the one who prays in me day and night. My stammerings are prayer: simply calling you by your name, Jesus, fills our communion to the full.

You are the one who, every morning, slips on my finger the ring of the prodigal son, the ring of festival.

So why have I wavered so long? Have I 'exchanged the glory of God for something useless; have I left the spring of living water to build myself cracked cisterns that hold nothing?' (Jeremiah 2)

You have been seeking me unwearyingly. Why did I hesitate once again, asking for time to deal with my own affairs? Once I had set my hand to the plough, why did I look back? Without realising it, I was making myself unfit to follow you.

Yet, though I had never seen you, I loved you.

You kept on saying: live the little bit of the Gospel you have grasped. Proclaim my life. Light fire on the earth . . . You, follow me . . .

Until one day I understand: you were asking me to commit myself to the point of no return.

78